# Shelter
## from the
# Storm

A Divine Plan for Overcoming Strife and Division

## RICH SODERQUIST

WESTBOW
P R E S S®
A DIVISION OF THOMAS NELSON
& ZONDERVAN

WestBow Press books may be ordered through
booksellers or by contacting:

WestBow Press
A Division of Thomas Nelson & Zondervan
1663 Liberty Drive
Bloomington, IN 47403
www.westbowpress.com
1 (866) 928-1240

ISBN: 978-1-9736-4843-7 (sc)
ISBN: 978-1-9736-4844-4 (hc)
ISBN: 978-1-9736-4842-0 (e)

Library of Congress Control Number: 2018914635

Print information available on the last page.

WestBow Press rev. date: 12/21/2018

# DEDICATION

## My Dads

## Duane Forrest Soderquist and John Wesley Zull

Without your wisdom and guidance, none of this would have been possible. Thanks go out to all the family and friends who pushed me to see my dream realized. Special thanks to author Ralph Nelson Willett and his ever-helpful wife, Sherri, for their guidance and encouragement.

# CONTENTS

# INTRODUCTION

People are hurting, and the world needs love. In every nation in every corner of the earth, in every business, every church, and every home, someone is dealing with the effects of strife and division. Unfortunately, few escape the grasp of its harm. Stress and its effects have been the silent health killer in our society for many years now—ask any doctor. Marital discord is a leading cause cited for divorce. Church boards and businesses often struggle with difficult personality conflicts. Nations fight nations, and Congress can't agree on much other than a pay raise.

This book is an easy read with an emphasis on eliminating strife and division in our lives. The Word of God reveals many encouraging details that, when applied correctly, help eliminate these difficulties. God did not intend for you to struggle through life, constantly dealing with division. Thank you for joining me as we journey through a simple four-point process to define, explore, eliminate, and control strife and divisions in our lives.

# CHAPTER 1

# Define It

# What Are Strife and Division?

B ob and Mary had been married for more than twenty years and knew all the right buttons to push in an argument. This one was no different. Bob came home from work early; he was out of gas and needed cash quick, but they found none. They spoke harsh words, and soon the house fell silent to a couple divided.

How many times have you been in a similar situation and thought, *Why, Lord, did this even happen? It was over nothing.*

A young college student could not get along with one of her new professors; for one, she could not understand his foreign dialect, and it was hard to understand his lectures. Then there was the constant belittling of the American way of life. Unless something changed quickly, she feared failure. This is a real example of two cultures thrown together with differing opinions—maybe right or maybe wrong, but divided none the less.

The church was everything Robbin had wanted in a worship experience since she had been a little girl. There was only one problem: the music—*and* it was too loud.

Robbin had been raised on traditional hymns, and she so loved the older songs. Nana had already expressed her opinion about the loud music. Michelle, Robbin's thirteen-year-old daughter, loved it—and for the first time in her life, she was responding to the Holy Spirit in a worship service. But could Robbin ever get used to this noise? Her worst thought was to leave and do it quickly. How could she ever tell the pastor?

The offense his brother had caused him years ago haunted him as he looked over his now dead brother's casket. Forgiveness and reconciliation face-to-face were no longer options because he was gone forever. Words were left unspoken for too long. If he could only tell his brother one last time that he was sorry for the silly things said in anger that now seemed so pointless.

The volleyball game was not that important—what was eating Carol was that her child had ridden the pine all year long while the rich kids played on. Could she ever forgive this coach for the negative effects not participating would have on her child?

Bobbie was not surprised when he arrived home from school and his mom and dad were fighting—Mom was bleeding, and Dad was black and blue and passed out on the kitchen floor. Bob had seen it all before; he never even slowed down as he grabbed a snack and went straight to his room to watch old black-and-white Laurel and Hardy films. The TV was his only friend, and he wondered if he would ever escape. Bob's parents had had a case-a-day beer habit since he was born; part of him wondered why he should even try differing from them.

Sex before marriage never bothered Sharon; after all, someone had abused her since childhood and used her at every turn. This time was different—it was her third abortion, and she was wondering about how this would affect her later in life. Could she ever forgive herself or anyone else?

Seeing yourself and others in these examples is easy; we've all experienced strife and division in our lives, and they leave no one out. The hard part is what to do about it and what we can change to make life better.

The book you're holding will give you four easy steps to handle division:

- **Defining it.** (Understanding the situation.)
- **Exploring it.** (Discovering what God's Word has to say on the subject.)
- **Eliminating it.** (Admitting, committing, and fully releasing our needs to God's care.)
- **Controlling our emotions surrounding it.** (Resisting negative thought patterns.)

I base the upcoming chapters on what the Bible has to say about the subject of strife and division. Before we go too far, let's define what strife and division are and are not.

Two distinct definitions from *Webster's Dictionary* (1828) explain it perfectly:

> **Division:** Disunion; discord; variance; difference.
> There was a **division** among the people.
> —John 7:43

> **Strife:** Contention in anger or enmity; contest; struggle for victory; quarrel or war.
> I and my people were at great **strife** with the children of Ammon.
> —Judges 12:2

Here are several top definitions of *division* from a 1913 edition of *Webster's*:

> The act or process of dividing anything into parts, or the state of being so divided; separation.

> That which divides or keeps apart; a partition.

> Disunion; difference in opinion or feeling; discord; variance; alienation.

> Divided opinions or interests, separation, disagreement, disunity, being divided, etc.

No matter how you define it, the results are usually negative.

The definition of *division* is something I studied for a very long time. To divide in mathematics is to split into equal parts or groups. Mathematics made me think that each time division takes place, you end up with less. Exceptions exist, but most division equals less of something.

Personal, professional, and spiritual divisions are no different; where there is division, there is less of everything. This is what's happening regularly when we allow division in our homes, marriages, and businesses—and yes, in our churches. Disunity runs through it all when division takes root. Add in strife, and we have a recipe for disaster.

*Webster's* defines *strife* as another form of division or separation. The Bible is clear on this issue, stating in James 3:16, "For where envying and strife is, there is confusion and every evil work."

Just like love will open the door to healing and forgiveness, strife will open the door to pain and suffering. The world is hurting, and as the saying goes, hurting people hurt people. Disagreements are everywhere; people want their rights and will fight for them. From the schoolyard to where we work, someone teaches people to stand their ground, to not give up without a fight, and to never let them see you cry. Virtues can be good, but when taken to extremes, they can become very harmful. This combative nature is contrary to the Spirit of God, and often people fail to recognize that Satan has used strife and division to get a foothold. Satan has used this tactic in humans' lives since he first stirred up trouble. God's plan is the opposite of this. The Spirit pours out His love so you can have an abundant life with less stress.

The following chart shows a great example of life lived through the Holy Spirit, and it compares it to the life lived without the Holy Spirit. The further you move away from the Spirit of God's direction, the closer you get to trouble and things contrary to His plans for your well-being.

| Life in the Holy Spirit =Abundant Life | Life without the Holy Spirit =Strife and Division |
|---|---|
| Loving............................ | ...............................Hateful |
| Joyful............................ | ........Depressed/miserable |
| Peaceful........................ | ...............Stressed/anxious |
| Patient.......................... | ........Frustrated with others |
| Kind.............................. | ....................Mean-spirited |
| Good............................. | ...................Evil/destructive |
| Faithful......................... | ...............................Corrupt |
| Gentle........................... | .................Harsh/uncaring |
| Self-controlled............ | ...........................Powerless |

Chart courtesy of Milan Bittenbender, pastor Life Bridge Church (South Haven, Michigan). Used by permission.

Not everything related to strife is caused by the devil. Satan will use whatever he can to divide us, but truth be told, sometimes we are to blame. Take a hard look in the mirror and ask yourself whether you could be doing something wrong. The blame game is alive and well, and we often blame others for our own shortcomings.

Regardless of how we let division take root, the facts are clear. Strife is a bad deal. You can easily see why we need help in this area. Exploring where God stands can get us on the right path.

# Key Takeaways from Chapter 1

- **Define it.** Name your need. (In this case, it's overcoming strife and division.)
- Strife and division are not God's plan.
- Satan will use division against you.

# Notes

# Notes

# CHAPTER 2

# Explore It
# What Does the Word Say?

The Bible teaches us in Isaiah that God is our creator and our source for everything; it tells us that we should rely on Him. God is Lord of all.

So that from the rising of the sun

to the place of its setting

people may know there is none besides me.

I am the Lord, and there is no other.

I form the light and create darkness,

I bring prosperity and create disaster;

I, the Lord, do all these things.

"You heavens above, rain down my righteousness;

let the clouds shower it down.

Let the earth open wide,

let salvation spring up,

let righteousness flourish with it;

> I, the Lord, have created it.
>
> —Isaiah 45:6–8 NIV

According to James 1:17 (NIV), all good gifts are from the Lord: "Every good and perfect gift comes from above."

The Lord reveals these things through scripture so that you understand that He is our guide. God wants us to follow His playbook in the form of the Bible, and He wants us to apply the Word to our daily walks—but how?

The easy road is to escalate an argument or join in on the gossip; it's easy to do anything but act in love. But is this what Christ would want for us? Certainly not. Consider Matthew 5:9 (NIV): "Blessed are the peacemakers, for they will be called children of God."

Driving it home further is Isaiah. The Lord's peace will never end:

> For unto us a child is born, unto us a son is given: and the government shall be upon his shoulder: and his name shall be called Wonderful, Counsellor, the mighty God, the everlasting Father, the Prince of Peace.
>
> Of the increase of his government and peace there shall be no end, upon the throne of David, and upon his kingdom, to order it, and to establish it with judgment and with

justice from henceforth even for ever. The
zeal of the Lord of hosts will perform this.
—Isaiah 9:6–7

Jesus loves me, and He loves you. So if we serve a risen
Savior who came as and remains the Prince of Peace,
and if we are blessed as peacemakers, then why would
we take any other road?

So how did we get here? How did the world arrive at such
a place in time where everything seems upside down?
The answer lies between good and evil and where we
stand on these subjects. It is very hard to have a serious
discussion about eliminating strife and division in any area
without discussing right standing before God. I define
right standing for this discussion as being redeemed and
making sure you're going to heaven through the gift of
eternal life through acceptance and belief in our savior
Jesus Christ. The Word of God shows that our hope should
be in our savior Jesus Christ. The ways to overcome
problems are through following the Bible's advice and
learning about God's guidance through the Holy Spirit.
The whole concept of salvation, God the Father, Jesus
the Son, and the Holy Spirit known as the Trinity may be
new to you, and that's okay. Only understand that Jesus
is seeking a relationship with you and longs to show you
His love.

Having fellowship with God, developing a personal
relationship with His Son Jesus Christ, and studying
the Word allow us as believers to exercise our faith and

explore this subject of the Holy Spirit further as we grow in our understanding of God's Word, the Bible. The Holy Spirit is our guide and an enormous part of salvation. The Bible is clear on the topic called the Trinity. God the Father, His son Jesus Christ, and our guide the Holy Spirit are the same but play different roles in our spiritual journey. This book is not a study of the Trinity, and many superb works exist on the subject. I mention this here as it is part of having a relationship with God. Those who apply the Word of God to their lives and rely on the Holy Spirit's direction are less likely to fall victim to the plans of the devil.

The question must be asked: Are you separated from God? Do you have a relationship with His Son? Do you want to know more about the Holy Spirit?

Separation is one of the main definitions of *division*. Humans separate naturally for several reasons, including marriage, death, divorce, jobs, and school. Some reasons are good, some bad. Take college, for instance: Leaving home for any reason can be fun and exciting. Traveling and going off to college can be some of the most exciting things we experience as humans. When you're separated from others, the feeling you get when you return home should be one of peace and relaxation. This is usually normal. Unfortunately, not all homes are peaceful these days, and for some, coming home is nothing but stressful. Family strife can take its toll.

The evil in this world will use anything to get to you and keep you from being connected to God. Satan has used our homes and relationships as a playground of strife for far too long.

Homes are meant to be sanctuaries of peace. Therefore, a right relationship with Jesus our Lord and Savior is so important.

Before we go too much further, we need to establish who you are in Christ and where you stand. Do you have a relationship with Jesus? It is very important for everyone to study salvation in Christ Jesus to make an informed decision.

The established Christian should also study this and be ready to witness and help those in need who have questions about salvation. God never intended for His creation (you) to be separated from Himself. Therefore, He sent His one and only Son to earth so you and I could live an eternal life in heaven.

Jesus was born, lived, was crucified, died, and was raised from the dead for everyone. There is so much more than separation that God intended for us through His son Jesus. Just like the college student or traveler returning home to a happy environment, Jesus wants you to return home to the family of God and a peaceful situation. The book of Romans shows us that salvation is for everyone:

> During the days of Jesus' life on earth, he offered up prayers and petitions with fervent cries and tears to the one who could save him from death, and he was heard because of his reverent submission. Son though he was, he learned obedience from what he suffered and, once made perfect, he became the source of eternal salvation for all who obey him and was designated by God to be high priest in the order of Melchizedek.
> —Romans 5:7–10 (NIV)

God allowed His Son to go to the cross for your sins. This should be a cause for shouting and celebration for everyone reading this book. Salvation is your first step to unity in Christ, your life, and all you do. God the Father desires to know you, and this is accomplished through His Son. Salvation takes place when a person listens to the salvation message, believes it, and receives Jesus into his or her heart, and God sends the Holy Spirit to live in you. The books of John and Romans say it so well.

> Jesus answered and said to him, "Most assuredly, I say to you, unless one is born again, he cannot see the kingdom of God."
> —John 3:3 (NIV)

> That if you confess with your mouth the Lord Jesus and believe in your heart that

God has raised Him from the dead, you will
be saved.
—Romans 10:9 (NIV)

This truly is the first step to combating strife and division in
your life. The promises of the Bible are true and accessible
for you. Those who make the decision in their heart to
follow Him are given the gift of eternal life in heaven.
Salvation is by grace, through faith—God's unmerited
favor. There's nothing you did or ever can do to deserve
it. It's a gift from God. All you must do is receive it!

The steps are simple. Follow them when you are ready to
enter this relationship.

> Dear Lord Jesus,
>
> Thank you for dying on the cross for my
> sin. Please forgive me for my sins. I repent
> of all of them. Come into my life. I receive
> you as my Lord and Savior. Now, please
> take control of my life and help me live for
> you forever.
>
> In the name of Jesus, I pray.
>
> Amen.

If you prayed this prayer, the Bible teaches that you were
born again. Now seal the deal, tell someone about your
decision. This does two things: it allows you to verbalize
your decision, and it makes your confession public. The
decision will become secure in your mind, and when

Satan tries to bring doubt your way, you will remember the day you made your decision and combat his lies. Satan comes to steal the Word of God. He will bring pressure, but God is great, and He is now your defender. Having the Holy Spirit living in your heart allows you to do all things from a place of peace and rest. Therefore, this first step of confession is vital. It sets you on a journey with God the Father, Jesus the Son, and the Holy Spirit.

The Word of God in 1 Corinthians 6:19–20 tells us that our bodies are the temple of the Holy Spirit.

> What? know ye not that your body is the temple of the Holy Ghost which is in you, which ye have of God, and ye are not your own?
>
> For ye are bought with a price: therefore glorify God in your body, and in your spirit, which are God's.

You don't have to walk this earth alone. God in the form of the Holy Spirit is now living in you. Jesus has promised He will never leave you or forsake you. Praise God! You're no longer designed for the world; you're designed to be a world overcomer.

> I have told you these things, so that in me you may have peace. In this world you will have trouble. But take heart! I have overcome the world.
> —John 16:33 (NIV)

Greater is he that is in you than he that is
in the world.
—1 John 4:4 (NIV)

You and God are now partners on a journey of faith.

Salvation more than anything we can do allows us to combat strife and division as the Word of God becomes alive to us. The promises of the Bible are now yours to discover and use on your journey. This may seem like a small thing now, but just consider this Bible verse as an example:

Be strong and courageous. Do not be
afraid; do not be discouraged, for the Lord
your God will be with you wherever you go.
—Joshua 1:9 (NIV)

Freedom is the name of the game now that you're saved. The freedom found in Christ is exciting and life-giving. Salvation is a life-changing experience. No longer are you in bondage to fear; you have accepted the truth, and the truth has set you free from sin and death. God is with you always and is accessible through prayer. The Word of God in the form of the Holy Bible is our guide to overcoming life's troubles and recurring fears. The next chapter will show the power the Word of God can have in your life. Chances are good you will see yourself in these situations.

The Bible has a lot to say about where God stands on strife, and He did not sacrifice His Son so we could be victims to its bondage. Colossians 1 tells us Christ's plan for us is to live a life of peace. Please think about that statement: you are a child of God and a vessel of peace. You are designed to operate in love and be at peace through the Holy Spirit. Take the time to apply what you discover as we unpack the next chapter.

# Key Takeaways from Chapter 2

- **Explore it.** Find out what the Word has to say about the subject so you can commit it to the Lord (in this case, overcoming strife and division).
- God is our creator and author of life.
- A right relationship with God is key for controlling strife and division.
- Salvation in Christ Jesus brings the Bible alive for the reader.

# Notes

# Notes

CHAPTER 3

# Eliminating It

Hopefully, you're on a journey with the Lord after reading the first part of this book. The principles taught here are 100 percent dependent on a relationship with our Lord and Savior Jesus Christ. Now that a personal relationship with God is a real thing for you—or, with established Christians, a renewed commitment to seek God's will—we can move forward to eliminating strife.

Discovering you have a need, as simple as that sounds, is the first step to eliminating it. Before you can develop a strategy, you must identify the issue.

You must name that opportunity for improvement, whether it's weight loss, trouble on the job, or in this case, removing division. This is the first step: you *admit* that it's real and needs attention. This is where many people fail; they will not admit they have a problem. Don't be that person. Tell the Lord that you have an issue. How do we communicate this need with God? Humans communicate with God through prayer. The Bible gives us a very clear path and direction to follow in scripture. You must pray. Bring your needs before the Lord. Ask, seek, and knock.

> Ask and it will be given to you; seek and you
> will find; knock and the door will be opened
> to you. For everyone who asks receives; the
> one who seeks finds; and to the one who
> knocks, the door will be opened. Which of
> you, if your son asks for bread, will give him
> a stone?
> —Matthew 7:7–12 (NIV)

Make your requests known to God and He will direct your path. Let's establish a pattern for a successful prayer life before we go further.

First things first: I'm not saying this is the only way to pray or that it will become your established pattern. I like this prayer especially during strife, while battling division, or while facing a serious situation that needs peace. The Lord hears our prayers whether they are quick, short, long, or any other variety. I believe He answers them and longs to fellowship with you. Pray in your own style, and don't be afraid to pour your heart out, especially if you're new to praying.

I want the best when I come before the Lord in prayer; we all want to find the right answers and to present our needs in a correct, successful way. Over several years of fellowship and prayer time, I have developed a system that works for my prayer life, especially during times of division. This is the basic prayer formula I use: acknowledge God, for me this means saying hello; praise Him; ask for forgiveness of any sin in your life that may come between you and your relationship with God or others; present your request, ideally based on what the Word says about your situation; thank Him and then close the prayer in His name: "In Jesus's name, amen."

A main part of this style of prayer is being in right standing with God and knowing what the Word says on the topic you are praying about. Get right with God before you pray. To me, this means asking God to forgive me if I have sinned or caused anyone strife. I keep a close watch on my behavior and check it often; I do this because, just as your personal family life can be strained, so can your walk with Christ when you have done something wrong. You can fall out of fellowship due to sin in your life, and it's important to make sure you seek forgiveness from God and others to eliminate strained relationships. My prayer life is so much richer just by starting out acknowledging that God is in control, praising Him, and asking the Lord of All to forgive me and set me straight before I pray out my needs. I love coming before Him with thanksgiving and making sure there is nothing between us that could negatively affect myself or others. I prefer to ask forgiveness of any sins or known offenses before praying. I base this in part on the wisdom found in Mark:

> Jesus replied to them, "Have faith in God. I assure you: If anyone says to this mountain, 'Be lifted up and thrown into the sea,' and does not doubt in his heart, but believes that what he says will happen, it will be done

for him. Therefore I tell you, all the things you pray and ask for—believe that you have received them, and you will have them. And whenever you stand praying, if you have anything against anyone, forgive him, so that your Father in heaven will also forgive you your wrongdoing. But if you don't forgive, neither will your Father in heaven forgive your wrongdoing."
—Mark 11:22–26 (HCSB)

Forgiving others and yourself of any wrongdoing is not to be confused with salvation. When we ask Christ to forgive our sins, we are redeemed—we are a part of God's family and have eternal life. Repeatedly asking for our sins to be forgiven to enter heaven is not what I'm referring to here. The forgiveness God purchased for you by Christ's atonement for your sin frees you from the threat of eternal condemnation. God has welcomed you into His family.

I would like to point out to those who are new in the faith or who just starting out in their relationship: do not worry or be overwhelmed. This is an example of what works for me. If this seems overwhelming, just pray, and God will help you sort it out. The Lord is looking out for you and desires to hear your prayers no matter what. A close relationship with Christ is something to be sought by everyone, and it starts with prayer.

This is a great place to review forgiveness. Jesus calls us to a lifestyle of peace, and being quick to forgive is a virtue.

Prayer, life, and relationships are just better when we are walking in love and forgiveness. But forgiveness can be a challenge. The word *forgiveness* sends fear through some people's minds and instant happiness through others'.

Forgiveness starts with being vulnerable and goes against the grain of the natural world. Being vulnerable has risks, but sometimes we must be vulnerable anyway. We naturally want to fight, usually for our rights. The natural way wants to blame the other guy—it was their fault. The devil will do anything he can to keep us from forgiveness and will distort the truth of God's Word at every possible chance. This is a lie straight from hell; staying in unforgiveness will keep you in the bondage of strife forever.

Jesus's example in the parable of the unmerciful servant should call us to action in our lives:

> Then came Peter to him, and said, Lord, how oft shall my brother sin against me, and I forgive him? till seven times?

> Jesus saith unto him, I say not unto thee, Until seven times: but, Until seventy times seven.

> Therefore is the kingdom of heaven likened unto a certain king, which would take account of his servants.

And when he had begun to reckon, one was brought unto him, which owed him ten thousand talents.

But forasmuch as he had not to pay, his lord commanded him to be sold, and his wife, and children, and all that he had, and payment to be made.

The servant therefore fell down, and worshipped him, saying, Lord, have patience with me, and I will pay thee all.

Then the lord of that servant was moved with compassion, and loosed him, and forgave him the debt.

But the same servant went out, and found one of his fellowservants, which owed him an hundred pence: and he laid hands on him, and took him by the throat, saying, Pay me that thou owest.

And his fellowservant fell down at his feet, and besought him, saying, Have patience with me, and I will pay thee all.

And he would not: but went and cast him into prison, till he should pay the debt.

So when his fellowservants saw what was done, they were very sorry, and came and told unto their lord all that was done.

Then his lord, after that he had called him, said unto him, O thou wicked servant, I forgave thee all that debt, because thou desiredst me:

Shouldest not thou also have had compassion on thy fellowservant, even as I had pity on thee?

And his lord was wroth, and delivered him to the tormentors, till he should pay all that was due unto him.

So likewise shall my heavenly Father do also unto you, if ye from your hearts forgive not every one his brother their trespasses.
—Matthew 18:21–35

True forgiveness is not from the head; this forgiveness is from the heart. Christ-like action must come from the heart. Forgiveness is something only you can do; it is not for your family, your friends, or others to complete. This is an individual action that only you can do, and it is key to eliminating division.

That argument you had with your spouse? You guessed it: only you can forgive your spouse. The boss who is such a jerk? Yes, only you can forgive. That's why it is so hard for people to go through with it. True forgiveness is hard, but we are called to be quick to forgive.

Monday came as a Monday this week, if you know what I mean. My wife and I had a character-building day when our daughter's truck had a catastrophic frame failure, her muffler broke off, and the brakes went out on our truck. Two vehicles broke down at once. I felt like I was in a country song. Being the human couple we are, we argued all the way home, and there was no peace until we forgave each other. I mention this to show you that it happens to us all, and that you must be ready to settle it or, trust me, it will settle you. Not forgiving will eat you alive.

Stop what you're doing and settle whatever you need to settle ASAP to avoid strife. Don't open the door—not even a crack.

I know that there are many hurting people with real deep-seated issues of abuse and neglect who find forgiveness almost impossible—just the thought of forgiving others for what they have done sends them into a panic attack. But Christ tells us this is the path to our personal freedom from the effects of sin. His words ring true and should be an inspiration to us all as we struggle with the tough things this life can throw at us.

Remember: God sent His Son to die for you; you have worth and value. God has invested a lot in you, and you have a life to live. Forgive the people who have hurt you, and forgive them now. The anointing of God allows us to complete this; it is through Him that all things are possible. God created you to be bold and to feel safe. He did not create you to be full of fear and worry.

> "No weapon that is formed against you will succeed; and every tongue that rises against you in judgment you will condemn. This [peace, righteousness, security, and triumph over opposition] is the heritage of the servants of the Lord, and this is their vindication from Me," says the Lord.
> —Isaiah 54:17 (AMP)

I know many of you are thinking, *If I forgive people, won't I become a doormat for everyone to step on?* No. Remember, you were not given a spirit of fear but one of power and a sound mind. Forgiveness does not reduce your strength; it increases it because you are operating from a place of right standing with God.

> For God did not give us a spirit of timidity or cowardice or fear, but [He has given us a spirit] of power and of love and of sound judgment and personal discipline [abilities that result in a calm, well-balanced mind and self-control].
> —2 Timothy 1:7 (AMP)

Set boundaries and let the spirit guide you. You are joint heirs with Jesus. Being secure is a blood-bought right you have inherited through Christ. Be daring in your prayers. Say about yourself what God says about you in the Bible. You're forgiven and loved. Practice loving and forgiving others. This is a freeing lifestyle.

The Word of God holds your identity. Speak it out of your mouth; your worth and value come from Christ. God loves you with an unconditional love, so act like it.

Serious emotional and physical struggles are what God specializes in fixing. One way He does this is through pastors, Christian psychologists, counselors, doctors, and support groups. Should you need professional services, these are the places to turn. I do not intend this book to replace professional help. Seek advice from those rooted in the medical and biblical perspective of healing. I encourage you to reach out to a trusted counselor and seek professional help for all serious emotional needs.

The great thing about following Christ is that He meets you where you're at, so whether you have major dilemmas or a day-to-day situation, He cares. He loves and cares for everything going on in your life. Forgiveness opens the door to your heart and to God's blessings. Always seek peace through forgiveness as you pray and overcome strife.

As we continue in our prayer example, establishing what the Word says is of utmost importance. The Bible drives this home in Philippians, calling us to take what we have learned from the Bible and put it into practice. Let your prayers be known to the Lord.

> Rejoice in the Lord always. I will say it again: Rejoice! Let your gentleness be evident to all. The Lord is near. Do not be anxious about anything, but in every situation, by prayer and petition, with thanksgiving, present your requests to God. And the peace of God, which transcends all understanding, will guard your hearts and your minds in Christ Jesus.
>
> Finally, brothers and sisters, whatever is true, whatever is noble, whatever is right, whatever is pure, whatever is lovely, whatever is admirable—if anything is excellent or praiseworthy—think about such things. Whatever you have learned or received or heard from me, or seen in me— put it into practice. And the God of peace will be with you.
> —Philippians 4:4–9 (NIV)

Find out what the Word says so you can properly commit the situation into His care through prayer based on His Word. The key to eliminating strife, division, and any kind of separation in your life is the proper application of God's Word in the form of the Holy Bible. The Word of God and what it says are of utmost importance for the study of any discipline, especially if one is to excel in the task at hand.

Those who have needs must be able to activate their faith, pray, and expect God to answer their prayers. The Bible is very clear on this; you have not because you ask not. Study! Right motives and preparation improve success in our walk with God.

> What causes fights and quarrels among you? Don't they come from your desires that battle within you? You desire but do not have, so you kill. You covet but you cannot get what you want, so you quarrel and fight. You do not have because you do not ask God. When you ask, you do not receive, because you ask with wrong motives, that you may spend what you get on your pleasures.

> You adulterous people, don't you know that friendship with the world means enmity against God? Therefore, anyone who chooses to be a friend of the world becomes an enemy of God. Or do you think Scripture says without reason that he jealously longs for the spirit he has caused to dwell in us? But he gives us more grace. That is why Scripture says:

> "God opposes the proud but shows favor to the humble."

Submit yourselves, then, to God. Resist the devil, and he will flee from you. Come near to God and he will come near to you. Wash your hands, you sinners, and purify your hearts, you double-minded. Grieve, mourn and wail. Change your laughter to mourning and your joy to gloom. Humble yourselves before the Lord, and he will lift you up.

Brothers and sisters, do not slander one another. Anyone who speaks against a brother or sister or judges them speaks against the law and judges it. When you judge the law, you are not keeping it, but sitting in judgment on it. There is only one Lawgiver and Judge, the one who is able to save and destroy. But you—who are you to judge your neighbor?
—James 4 (NIV)

You must slow down, study the Word to find out what it says, and then apply it to your situation if you ever expect to walk in victory over life's complications. This is one of the most difficult things for some people to do, as it takes time and effort and is contrary to what the fast-paced world teaches. The world says everything should happen quickly. Humans live in a world of instant everything, including soup, rice, and directions. Commercials tell us to worry about everything, and this fear is mixed with the headline news every day. Combine this with instant, nonstop communications, and you can see how people misunderstand each other and have trouble overcoming division.

The norm is to do everything on your own, do it quickly, and not rely on God's direction. This must stop if we are to overcome division! Have you ever noticed that the best answers to life's problems are not instant fixes but long-term solutions? This is the same for eliminating all forms of strife. The Lord can instantaneously take away our problems and often does this when we pray. But just as often, it is something we need to walk out over time. The good news is that He always walks with us and never leaves us. Obedience to the will of God brings positive results, and the way to tap into this is by consistent application of the Holy Scripture. Cast your cares onto the Lord.

> Cast all your anxiety on him because he cares for you.
> —1 Peter 5:7 (NIV)

This is the second step to eliminating strife and division: *commit* the problem to God. The following verses are just a sample of what the Bible has to say about strife, division, and how to eliminate them from all areas of our journey. The book of Romans, the Psalms, and Proverbs are awesome resources for us to study and memorize. Memorizing scripture is biblical and will help you when strife rears its ugly head. The Bible is not always handy, but what's memorized in your head and heart will come out of your mouth, good or bad. Proverbs 7 calls us to bind these to our heart.

> My son, keep my words
>
> and store up my commands within you.
>
> Keep my commands and you will live;
>
> guard my teachings as the apple of your eye.
>
> Bind them on your fingers;
>
> write them on the tablet of your heart.
>
> Say to wisdom, "You are my sister,"
>
> and to insight, "You are my relative."
>
> —Proverbs 7:1–4 (NIV)

Who's the apple of your eye? Understand that this is most likely a family member or a good friend. The Word of God often uses references of the relationships with our family to drive home the point of the verse. This is because Jesus's goal is for all of us to be a family. This is a true picture of His love for all mankind. Remember, Satan came to kill, steal, and destroy; Christ came that you would have life in abundance. Satan's plan is anything but family or love.

> The thief comes only to steal and kill and destroy; I have come that they may have life, and have it to the full.
>
> —John 10:10 (NIV)

While writing this book, I had to look this verse up. I should have it written on the tablet of my heart. See how important it is to apply these verses regularly, so you can share with your friends, family, and strangers? Share the love of God. God wants you to have self-control through study and application of biblical principles. God's Word puts a high regard on this skill.

> Better a patient person than a warrior, one
> with self-control than one who takes a city.
> —Proverbs 16:32 (NIV)

In this verse, we discover how important it is to have power over ourselves through Christ. Better than being a warrior and conquering a whole city! God always provides direction in His Word and ability through Him to apply the fix for our needs. Many verses throughout the Bible are related, containing direction and application. Just like me and my sister, whom I deeply admire, respect, and love for her guidance, they are related and loved verses. God would never give us an example to better ourselves and then not provide direction on how to excel in that area. Proverbs, for example, tells us to be in control, and Romans tells us how. This allows us to overcome things like anger, arguing, wrong thoughts, and unwanted negative emotions through the Word. Choose life in the Word and you will naturally choose a life headed in the right direction. Turning from negative to positive as you apply the Word to your situations will eliminate strife and division. This is best accomplished by imitating God's love and showing love in all we do.

The first thing we want to do in any troublesome situation is take charge. Everyone wants to fix the problem, charge in with guns blazing, save the damsel in distress, and wrap our problem up in thirty minutes—after all, every sitcom on TV does. Why can't we?

This can be an especially trying situation when our children, spouse, significant other, and family are concerned. Rushing in with guns blazing is seldom the answer. Seriously consider your last big problem. Did it take a few hours, days, months, or years to resolve? I'm writing this, and I took five months to get in to see an ear, nose, and throat specialist. Finally, I know what course of action to take. The key is knowing God has your back. He's got this.

How about your boss or that tough job situation? One of my tough job situations took over ten years to resolve— that was a long, tense relationship. You get my point: God answers prayer, but sometimes it takes patience. It's tough in a microwave world where we sit in front of the control and think, *Hurry, I don't have all minute to wait!* Waiting and being patient are not real popular answers but are often key to dealing with those things causing stress from division. Remember one of our definitions of *division* is "not agreeing."

Remember the last time you rushed into an argument because you were tired or jumped to conclusions without all the facts. This is strife's playground, and misunderstandings because of our lack of patience can come fast and hard. Trouble is often the result, leaving a wake of division between family and friends that can last a long time. I like to call this the two-by-four effect: we run headlong into the beam in the barn and wonder why our head hurts. Stop running into the beam. Stop rushing everything!

The wise person will avoid this rush at all costs and carefully and patiently consider how to handle disagreements.

> A person's wisdom yields patience; it is to
> one's glory to overlook an offense.
> —Proverbs 19:11 (NIV)

God calls us to be patient. God specifically calls us to be patient in trials. He does this on purpose, so we can become mature, lacking nothing. Maturity includes patience in how we act and how we respond to others. Do you rush to judgment, or slowly consider the facts when faced with difficult decisions? Grandmother's advice to hold your tongue and sleep on that big decision is still great advice.

Sometimes the Lord makes us wait. I know that's not what you want to hear, or even what's popular to preach these days, but it's true. Often, we are not mature enough to be trusted with certain things. Just as you would not trust a toddler with a steak knife, the Lord will give us only what we can handle and not let us harm ourselves. This can be a long process of growth, but just as the toddler grows to a teen who can carve the Thanksgiving turkey, so will you mature as a Christian if you study and apply the Word of God to your situation. This is a natural cycle of training.

Consider what James says about trials and temptations:

> Consider it pure joy, my brothers and sisters, whenever you face trials of many kinds, because you know that the testing of your faith produces perseverance. Let perseverance finish its work so that you may be mature and complete, not lacking anything.
> —James 1:2–4 (NIV)

The Lord's goal is for you to be complete, lacking nothing. This includes knowledge and wisdom. The Lord's plans for your life can be trusted, and He can take you further than you ever dreamed, but you must trust Him with your whole life.

Consider the rich young ruler:

> And a certain ruler asked him, saying, Good Master, what shall I do to inherit eternal life?

And Jesus said unto him, Why callest thou me good? none is good, save one, that is, God.

Thou knowest the commandments, Do not commit adultery, Do not kill, Do not steal, Do not bear false witness, Honour thy father and thy mother.

And he said, All these have I kept from my youth up.

Now when Jesus heard these things, he said unto him, Yet lackest thou one thing: sell all that thou hast, and distribute unto the poor, and thou shalt have treasure in heaven: and come, follow me.

And when he heard this, he was very sorrowful: for he was very rich.

And when Jesus saw that he was very sorrowful, he said, How hardly shall they that have riches enter into the kingdom of God!

For it is easier for a camel to go through a needle's eye, than for a rich man to enter into the kingdom of God.

And they that heard it said, Who then can be saved?

And he said, The things which are impossible with men are possible with God.

Then Peter said, Lo, we have left all, and followed thee.

And he said unto them, Verily I say unto you, There is no man that hath left house, or parents, or brethren, or wife, or children, for the kingdom of God's sake,

Who shall not receive manifold more in this present time, and in the world to come life everlasting.
—Luke 18:18–30

I firmly believe the rich young ruler would have gone on to bigger and better things if he would have just laid down the last portion of his life—his money—at the feet of Christ. The Lord could have easily improved his life, even if He chose not to increase him financially. The life He had planned for the ruler would have been so much more fulfilling and, I dare say, *rich*. God had watched over and blessed this man his whole life and loved him so much that He gave him a meeting with His Son Jesus Christ, hoping the man's life would be complete. This is a perfect story of how patient God is with us and how much He looks over us from the day we are born. God is patient with us, and His Son mimics this with His answer, not being upset with the ruler but pointing out that nothing is impossible with God. God wants us to learn to lean on Him heavily for our answers, and this is especially true for patience.

No one said this would be easy. Possible in Christ? Yes, but you must take the step and start speaking the Word in love over your situations. Take responsibility. Claim the scriptures. Make them your own in prayer, and God will back them up 150 percent. Learning to trust as we apply patience can be so tough, especially for those who seemingly have it all together. Remember this story in a new context as you practice patience in your life. God is in control. And remember: nothing is impossible with God.

> Those who live according to the flesh have their minds set on what the flesh desires; but those who live in accordance with the Spirit have their minds set on what the Spirit desires. The mind governed by the flesh is death, but the mind governed by the Spirit is life and peace.
> —Romans 8:5–6 NIV

Here we are called to be at peace through the Holy Spirit. This includes controlling strife in our life. Remember: through your own strength, you can't accomplish these commands, but with the Holy Spirit's help, you can more than a conquer. In Romans 8, the Word shows us that the Father's will for us is to ask and expect that He will graciously give us all things. This includes self-control, and He gives us the ability to grow in this area. We need only ask for it to become a reality in our lives! Hardship and trouble are overcome through the Word and prayer. Blessings are found as we roll our problems over to His care.

You are a precious child of God. Jesus loves you and has designed a life that should be free from bondage and from a nature always at odds with everything. God loves you so much that nothing can separate you from Him. The nature of God overcomes for us. Remember that God is always working on your behalf, and He wants desperately to have fellowship with you. God is interceding on your behalf right now, even as you read this chapter. This same God can be trusted with all your cares, including any caused by division, which brings us to step three: *eliminating it.* I call this *full release!* Releasing your cares to God is so important; it gives Him your permission to take it from you fully.

Admitting we had a problem and naming it gave us the thing that had to be dealt with in step one. Committing it to God by asking for His help based on scripture so we know we're on solid ground was step two. Step three gives it fully and permanently to Him, fully releasing strife into His care. By doing this, you are literally rolling the situation into His arms and releasing it from your care. This is where it gets tough, because as humans we like to hold on tight to our stuff, and that includes our problems. This is contrary to the Word of God, and we are called to permanently and fully release our cares onto Him.

> Cast all your anxiety on Him because He cares for you.
> —1 Peter 5:7 NIV

Remember this is a full release; you are never to pick it up again. The situation is now God's problem to deal with. You may pray and listen for more direction from the Holy Spirit about which direction to take, but never again will you wonder if God is working on it. You know He has it and it is His. He owns it now, and you are to respect that. Doing this can be so difficult for some people that I have included an entire chapter on controlling thoughts around this step.

> For in this hope we were saved. But hope that is seen is no hope at all. Who hopes for what they already have? But if we hope for what we do not yet have, we wait for it patiently.
>
> In the same way, the Spirit helps us in our weakness. We do not know what we ought to pray for, but the Spirit himself intercedes for us through wordless groans. And he who searches our hearts knows the mind of the Spirit, because the Spirit intercedes for God's people in accordance with the will of God.

And we know that in all things God works for the good of those who love him, who have been called according to his purpose. For those God foreknew he also predestined to be conformed to the image of his Son, that he might be the firstborn among many brothers and sisters. And those he predestined, he also called; those he called, he also justified; those he justified, he also glorified.
—Romans 8:24–30 NIV

Eliminating strife and division in all areas is a journey and a destination. Unfortunately, this can take years to accomplish—I'm just being very transparent here! Take my life, for example. There was a time when various habits had a hold on my life, including severe profanity. Every other word out of my mouth was a terrible word.

This was eventually eliminated through the Holy Spirit. Then one day, I woke up and realized I don't swear anymore. The need to swear every other word is gone forever. Can you guess when it is still an issue? You guessed it: when I'm stressed, strife rears its ugly head and I let a profanity slip in my human condition. What's the fix? The Word of God is the fix. Repent, pray, and move on.

The point is that eliminating this stuff on your own just doesn't work. However, with God, all things become possible. Therefore, the key to eliminating strife and division is to rely on God and His direction in your life. Grab hold of anything He offers as if it is a life preserver and you are lost at sea. Grab the Word, grab fellowship with other Christians, join a good church, watch uplifting shows, and listen to uplifting music. Fill your mind, heart, and time with things of God, and you will not have any time for the devil. This will allow you to resist him, and he will flee from you.

Being this serious about controlling strife may seem like going overboard, but this is your life we are talking about. To overcome, you must get serious about your walk with God. Does this mean you have to live a boring life without joy? No! No! Emphatically I say *no!* God's plans for you are so much bigger than your plans, and His will for you is so much bigger than you can ever imagine. Life with Him in control is a celebration every day. He made you and designed you, and that means if you want to excel and be a better nurse, doctor, lawyer, student, singer, friend, fisherman, YouTuber, social media guru, programmer, or whatever you want to become, He is all in for you. His mind is there for you, living inside you to give you witty inventions, or abilities to care for others and love your pastor, church members, family, and friends. You get the idea: Just love somebody today. Live a life of love, sharing the blessings. Live like there's no tomorrow, for He lives inside you and is your father. Amen and hallelujah. Shout out loud; I know I do. God loves me, and I love Him, and together mixed with love we are an unstoppable team! Fill your life with God, and you will be an unstoppable force to be reckoned with. God does not desire that His children be mired in strife and division. Vow to eliminate it through Christ today.

# Key Takeaways from Chapter 3

- **Eliminate it.** Full release. (Forever roll it into His care.)
- You are a precious child of God called to a life of peace.
- Love, patience, and forgiveness will help you be a strife overcomer. Walk in love.

# Notes

# Notes

CHAPTER 4

# Controlling Emotions Surrounding It

The foundational scripture for this chapter is Proverbs 3:21–22. The Message version of the Bible brings this verse alive for the reader:

> Dear friend, guard clear thinking and common sense with your life; don't for a minute lose sight of them. They'll keep your soul alive and well, they'll keep you fit and attractive.
> —Proverbs 3:2 (The Message)

Many books have been written about transforming the mind and controlling our thoughts. Great books such as these should be a part of everyone's library. I call upon them in a time of need to make sure I'm thinking straight.

The Bible calls us to become more Christ-like and to take every thought captive. This book echoes all these skills and yet differs from many books in print as it is a simple call to action, a just-get-it-done type of approach to our thoughts and actions concerning division. Bottom line: you must control your emotions. Hot-button issues will force your hand every time. Life on Earth is one continuous battle, and how you respond to tough situations can make or break your victory. The good news is that Christ has won the victory; you will have challenges, but remember, the Holy Spirit is always with you.

Everyone has a hot button and can easily take offense if provoked, discouraged, under stress, or carrying deep-seated beliefs. During a crisis or even during your daily routine, it is easy to let your thoughts and emotions rule instead of ruling them. Don't lose sight of a clear mind. How we react often depends on what is going on in our life or what is near and dear to our heart.

Therefore, the Christian must be very humble and patient with others. How Christ treats us is how we should treat others. Christ treats us in love, and we should treat others in love, and that includes how you treat yourself. Refrain from being too critical of yourself. The stress-free lifestyle void of strife is not possible without love. Walking in love is how believers gain victory over emotions.

This is one of the most profound things the Holy Spirit has revealed. Love wins over strife and division. Love wins over negative thought. Patience, love, and kindness unlock the door to the treasures of heaven. Love is the key to victorious living in Christ. Provision and all good things flow from and start with love.

We are called to be ambassadors of love. Everything we do, all our responses, should be based in and stem from love.

Basing all we do in love allows God to work on our behalf, frees up spiritual forces to action, and is the path of success. Control emotions with love, and do nothing out of fear. Operating in fear will wreak havoc on your emotions.

> But have nothing to do with foolish and ignorant speculations [useless disputes over unedifying, stupid controversies], since you know that they produce strife and give birth to quarrels. The servant of the Lord must not participate in quarrels, but must be kind to everyone [even-tempered, preserving peace], skilled in teaching, patient and tolerant when wronged. He must correct those who are in opposition with courtesy and gentleness in the hope that God may grant that they will repent and be led to the knowledge of the truth [accurately understanding and welcoming it], and that they may come to their senses and escape from the trap of the devil, having been held captive by him to do his will.
> —2 Timothy 2:23–26 (AMP)

One of my hot-button issues is organization—or lack thereof. Being a trained project manager and lean program specialist has its advantages, but the hot-button downside is that I like things in their place. Not overly neat—in their place and working.

Change is not always easy, even for a trained change agent like me. Imagine my surprise when I arrived home alone from church ready to relax and eat lunch after a great church service only to find a flood in our new kitchen. I had been on a spiritual high before this happened. I had just witnessed a great baptism service, victories, and answered prayers, and here sat a flood, wet wood, and disconnected plumbing.

The plumbing nuts had come loose from being hit by the garbage can as we repeatedly pulled it out and put it back over the years. Only God knows how long it had been disconnected. Did I mention the wet garbage and mouse stuff? Oh, there's nothing worse than mouse stuff. I go instantly into Destroy All Rodents mode, and this is a hot button for me too. I hate mice!

I dislike them so much that I had sealed every crack and had spent boatloads of money to keep them out of my new kitchen. So when I came home to a flooded kitchen, I was furious, and I'm sure I heard God laughing at me as I cleaned.

Do you think it tempted me to let discouragement take over? It would have been easy to blame myself, my spouse, or my children. I could have let this problem steal my peace, but it was just a challenge that was easily fixed in just three hours.

God wants you to have success as you tap into the Holy Spirit that lives in you as a believer. The believer is not given a spirit of fear but one of a sound mind, able to handle things that arise in peace and victory without strife. Consider Romans 8 and what it says about a life lived through the guidance of the Holy Spirit.

> There is therefore now no condemnation to them which are in Christ Jesus, who walk not after the flesh, but after the Spirit.
>
> For the law of the Spirit of life in Christ Jesus hath made me free from the law of sin and death.
>
> For what the law could not do, in that it was weak through the flesh, God sending his own Son in the likeness of sinful flesh, and for sin, condemned sin in the flesh:
>
> That the righteousness of the law might be fulfilled in us, who walk not after the flesh, but after the Spirit.
>
> For they that are after the flesh do mind the things of the flesh; but they that are after the Spirit the things of the Spirit.
>
> For to be carnally minded is death; but to be spiritually minded is life and peace.

Because the carnal mind is enmity against God: for it is not subject to the law of God, neither indeed can be.

So then they that are in the flesh cannot please God.

But ye are not in the flesh, but in the Spirit, if so be that the Spirit of God dwell in you. Now if any man have not the Spirit of Christ, he is none of his.

And if Christ be in you, the body is dead because of sin; but the Spirit is life because of righteousness.

But if the Spirit of him that raised up Jesus from the dead dwell in you, he that raised up Christ from the dead shall also quicken your mortal bodies by his Spirit that dwelleth in you.

Therefore, brethren, we are debtors, not to the flesh, to live after the flesh.

For if ye live after the flesh, ye shall die: but if ye through the Spirit do mortify the deeds of the body, ye shall live.

For as many as are led by the Spirit of God, they are the sons of God.

For ye have not received the spirit of bondage again to fear; but ye have received the Spirit of adoption, whereby we cry, Abba, Father.

The Spirit itself beareth witness with our spirit, that we are the children of God:

And if children, then heirs; heirs of God, and joint-heirs with Christ; if so be that we suffer with him, that we may be also glorified together.

For I reckon that the sufferings of this present time are not worthy to be compared with the glory which shall be revealed in us.

For the earnest expectation of the creature waiteth for the manifestation of the sons of God.

For the creature was made subject to vanity, not willingly, but by reason of him who hath subjected the same in hope,

Because the creature itself also shall be delivered from the bondage of corruption into the glorious liberty of the children of God.

For we know that the whole creation groaneth and travaileth in pain together until now.

And not only they, but ourselves also, which have the firstfruits of the Spirit, even we ourselves groan within ourselves, waiting for the adoption, to wit, the redemption of our body.

For we are saved by hope: but hope that is seen is not hope: for what a man seeth, why doth he yet hope for?

But if we hope for that we see not, then do we with patience wait for it.

Likewise the Spirit also helpeth our infirmities: for we know not what we should pray for as we ought: but the Spirit itself maketh intercession for us with groanings which cannot be uttered.

And he that searcheth the hearts knoweth what is the mind of the Spirit, because he maketh intercession for the saints according to the will of God.

And we know that all things work together for good to them that love God, to them who are the called according to his purpose.

For whom he did foreknow, he also did predestinate to be conformed to the image of his Son, that he might be the firstborn among many brethren.

Moreover whom he did predestinate, them he also called: and whom he called, them he also justified: and whom he justified, them he also glorified.

What shall we then say to these things? If God be for us, who can be against us?

He that spared not his own Son, but delivered him up for us all, how shall he not with him also freely give us all things?

Who shall lay any thing to the charge of God's elect? It is God that justifieth.

Who is he that condemneth? It is Christ that died, yea rather, that is risen again, who is even at the right hand of God, who also maketh intercession for us.

Who shall separate us from the love of Christ? shall tribulation, or distress, or persecution, or famine, or nakedness, or peril, or sword?

As it is written, For thy sake we are killed all the day long; we are accounted as sheep for the slaughter.

Nay, in all these things we are more than conquerors through him that loved us.

For I am persuaded, that neither death, nor life, nor angels, nor principalities, nor powers, nor things present, nor things to come,

Nor height, nor depth, nor any other creature, shall be able to separate us from the love of God, which is in Christ Jesus our Lord.
—Romans 8:1–39

Those who live according to the Spirit have their minds set on what the Spirit desires, including peace and freedom from sin and division and the trouble they cause. Most battles are fought in our heads. The mind and our thoughts can often be the difference between struggle and victory. The Bible states that we are to take control of our thoughts and cast down vain imaginations. Take control of what you are thinking always.

Why is this so important? Why would I write a book on this? The reason is simple: we are in a war, and many people fail to acknowledge it, let alone give it much thought. This is a life-and-death situation. Satan has one goal, and that's destroying you through any method possible. You are just another foe to be vanquished.

Sin is one of the easiest ways for Satan to develop strongholds that lead to death in your life. Wrong thinking will cause you to stray off course and, like a baby animal separated from its mother, you will become easy prey for the predator.

Don't believe me? Check out what the Word has to say about Satan's plan:

> Be alert and of sober mind. Your enemy the devil prowls around like a roaring lion looking for someone to devour.
> —1 Peter 5:8 (NIV)

The Christian must be strong and of good courage, taking advantage of the tools God has provided. Tools like His precious Word keep evil far from us and our loved ones. Put on the full armor of God and pray. This is a war, a war for your life and your peace. Stand firm and control your emotions.

> Finally, be strong in the Lord and in his mighty power. Put on the full armor of God, so that you can take your stand against the devil's schemes.
> —Ephesians 6:10–11 (NIV)

Remember those sister verses we studied? Check out Second Corinthians; it says we can demolish strongholds. The Word always gives us direction and the ability to overcome. Faithfulness is steadiness in Christ. Remain faithful to obeying the Word and prepare for victory.

> The weapons we fight with are not the weapons of the world. On the contrary, they have divine power to demolish strongholds. We demolish arguments and every pretension that sets itself up against the knowledge of God, and we take captive every thought to make it obedient to Christ.
> —2 Corinthians 10:4–5 (NIV)

Take your thoughts captive, and do this based on the Word. The believer must resist negative thoughts concerning the situations we bring to God. This is the last step in total victory over our battles: resistance to a negative attack strategy of the enemy called *doubt*. This book has lain the groundwork. We have named our problem, admitted our needs to God, committed them to Him in prayer, released them into His care, and now we must resist all attempts by the devil to steal our victory. Do not let doubt cloud your mind; resist negative thought or anything about your situation contrary to the Word of God. Resist the devil, and he will flee from you.

> Submit yourselves, then, to God. Resist the devil, and he will flee from you.
> —James 4:7 (NIV)

Resisting the devil is the key to not having your victory stolen. Remind yourself that God has your problem under control and that you have released it into His care. Remember that He has your back and is working the issue for you.

This is where many people get hung up, thinking this is a one-and-done effort. They ask themselves why they struggle with this as they roll the problem over and over in their mind. Keeping your mind stable is not a one-and-done event; it is a learned response. You must condition your mind to remain stable. This is essential to victory over our problems. The Bible shows great examples of this in several places, including the first book of Peter:

> Therefore, with your minds ready for action, be serious and set your hope completely on the grace to be brought to you at the revelation of Jesus Christ. As obedient children, do not be conformed to the desires of your former ignorance. But as the One who called you is holy, you also are to be holy in all your conduct; for it is written, Be holy, because I am holy.
> —1 Peter 1:13–16 (HCBS)

Do not let doubt and unbelief cloud your thoughts. Instead, be stable and steady. Think on the positive side of your thoughts and emotions. I love positive thinking and everything it can bring, but this is so much more than positive thinking. This is letting the Holy Spirit guide your emotions by learning to control your thoughts.

Control your thoughts and you control your emotions and stay stable. This is exactly what Paul was talking about when he said he *learned* to be content no matter what situation he was in. Philippians 4 lays it all out: he learned. This means he practiced and became proficient at being content. Believers must practice controlling their mind.

> I am not saying this because I am in need, for I have learned to be content whatever the circumstances. I know what it is to be in need, and I know what it is to have plenty. I have learned the secret of being content in any and every situation, whether well fed or hungry, whether living in plenty or in want. I can do all this through him who gives me strength.
> —Philippians 4:11–13 (NIV)

Paul also taught us in Philippians to dwell upon those things that are honorable, true, and worthy of praise. Thinking on these items helps us stay stable in thought. Stay stable, stay in love, and you have overcome strife and division. Let the strength of Christ guide your thoughts. Learn to control your emotions.

Continually use this book as a reference to gain the upper hand over strife and division. Make it a habit, just like brushing your teeth or shampooing your hair. Lather, rinse, and repeat. Christ cares for you and is working on your situation.

# Key Takeaways from Chapter 4

- **Control it.** Guard emotions. (Control your thoughts through the Holy Spirit.)
- You are loved, and nothing can separate you from Gods love.
- Through Christ you have a sound mind and were not given a spirit of fear. Walk in victory.

# Notes

# Notes

CHAPTER 5

# The Four-Step Elimination Process

## The four-step strife and division elimination process:

- **Define it.** Admit you have a need.
  (Father, help me overcome strife and division.)

- **Explore it.** Commit it to the Lord.
  (Father, I commit it to you.)

- **Eliminate it.** Full release.
  (Forever roll it into His care.)

- **Control your emotions surrounding it.** Resist the devil.
  (Take control of your thoughts.)

A nyone can use the four-step technique as a problem-solving tool for many applications, not just strife and division. Weight loss, for example, would be a good one to run through the system. For most of us, defining it would be as easy as looking at your last physical, but for grins, let's say you need to lose a few pounds safely.

Defining it will not be a problem. You could go online or talk to a doctor and in short order have the statistics on what losing a few pounds should look like for your gender, size, and shape. Definitions would include body size, base metabolic intake, and a hundred other facts on weight.

Exploring it further would reveal multiple books, diet plans, companies, and programs to help. Ask the Lord to help you and to continue to claim success through the scriptures.

Losing weight is difficult for me and, before I found prayer, would have been a different story for me. However, after trying several programs and techniques, I have found one that works for me. Simple lifestyle changes—eating when I'm hungry and stopping before I overeat—have been a big factor. So has drinking water, water, and more water.

Tonsil surgery helped me reduce weight and increase stamina as well. Sounds simple, but it took many years to discover the answer.

I had to keep praying, and I finally discovered a way to control my weight. The point is, don't give up; keep using tools such as this book and let the Lord guide you as you eliminate difficulties.

The process can also be used for other situations, such as discovering new talents. Building a garage or changing a light. Finding a new hobby or exercising. Run anything through the four-step process and it could help you discover the resources to do new things.

# Key Takeaways from Chapter 5

- **Live it.** Act. (Make God's word your final authority.)
- Pray and bring all your requests to God.
- Through Christ, God's word and prayer victory is always possible.

# Notes

# Notes

CHAPTER 6

# Epilogue

I wrote this book with a lot of inspiration from the Word of God. I find one of the main foundational passages for my outlook in 1 John 5 of the King James Version of the Bible. This chapter lays it all out for those struggling with any issue, and it includes everything needed for an abundant life: believe in Christ, get eternal life, be an overcomer, remember that God hears and answers our prayers, keep His commandments, love, and live.

I hope my writing will bring all the glory and praise to God, may change at least one life for the better, and will give you practical tools for spiritual growth. First Corinthians 12 explains that God desires there to be no division in the body. I pray that you have found a nugget of wisdom while reading this book.

Remember, division always equals less, and Satan is the divider; however, you are more than a conqueror through Christ Jesus.

In Christ,

Rich Soderquist

Whosoever believeth that Jesus is the Christ is born of God: and every one that loveth him that begat loveth him also that is begotten of him.

By this we know that we love the children of God, when we love God, and keep his commandments.

For this is the love of God, that we keep his commandments: and his commandments are not grievous.

For whatsoever is born of God overcometh the world: and this is the victory that overcometh the world, even our faith.

Who is he that overcometh the world, but he that believeth that Jesus is the Son of God?

This is he that came by water and blood, even Jesus Christ; not by water only, but by water and blood. And it is the Spirit that beareth witness, because the Spirit is truth.

For there are three that bear record in heaven, the Father, the Word, and the Holy Ghost: and these three are one.

And there are three that bear witness in earth, the Spirit, and the water, and the blood: and these three agree in one.

If we receive the witness of men, the witness of God is greater: for this is the witness of God which he hath testified of his Son.

He that believeth on the Son of God hath the witness in himself: he that believeth not God hath made him a liar; because he believeth not the record that God gave of his Son.

And this is the record, that God hath given to us eternal life, and this life is in his Son.

He that hath the Son hath life; and he that hath not the Son of God hath not life.

These things have I written unto you that believe on the name of the Son of God; that ye may know that ye have eternal life, and that ye may believe on the name of the Son of God.

And this is the confidence that we have in him, that, if we ask any thing according to his will, he heareth us:

And if we know that he hear us, whatsoever we ask, we know that we have the petitions that we desired of him.

If any man see his brother sin a sin which is not unto death, he shall ask, and he shall give him life for them that sin not unto death. There is a sin unto death: I do not say that he shall pray for it.

All unrighteousness is sin: and there is a sin not unto death.

We know that whosoever is born of God sinneth not; but he that is begotten of God keepeth himself, and that wicked one toucheth him not.

And we know that we are of God, and the whole world lieth in wickedness.

And we know that the Son of God is come, and hath given us an understanding, that we may know him that is true, and we are in him that is true, even in his Son Jesus Christ. This is the true God, and eternal life.

Little children, keep yourselves from idols. Amen.
—1 John 5

# Notes

# Notes

# ABOUT THE AUTHOR

Rich Soderquist is an author, photographer, videographer and web developer. He holds an MBA in business management and several professional certifications. Rich works in a variety of forums including Christian business and financial leadership, electronics education, project management and continuous improvement principles. Active in the Church for over thirty years he strives to bring education, training and unity where there is division. Rich loves everything fishing and enjoys being in the outdoors as often as possible. Rich lives in South Haven, Michigan with his wife and two daughters.

Printed in the United States
By Bookmasters